An
Oak
Hunch

Other Books by Phil Hall

The Bad Sequence (Book Thug, 2004)
Trouble Sleeping (Brick Books, 2000)
Hearthedral: A Folk-Hermetic (Brick Books, 1996)
The Unsaid (Brick Books, 1992)
Amanuensis (Brick Books, 1989)
Old Enemy Juice (Quarry Press, 1988)
Why I Haven't Written (Brick Books, 1985)
A Minor Operation (blewointment, 1984)
Homes (Black Moss, 1979)
Eighteen Poems (Cyanamid, 1973)

An
Oak
Hunch

Phil Hall

Brick Books

Library and Archives Canada Cataloguing in Publication

Hall, Phil
     An oak hunch / Phil Hall.

Poems.
ISBN 1-894078-44-6

     I. Title.

PS8565.A449O23 2005   C811'.54   C2005-903456-4

We acknowledge the support of the Canada Council for
the Arts, the Government of Canada through the Book
Publishing Industry Development Program (BPIDP), and
the Ontario Arts Council for their support of our
publishing program.

The book is set in Bembo.

Design and layout by Alan Siu.

Printed and bound by Sunville Printco Inc.

Brick Books
431 Boler Road, Box 20081
London, Ontario N6K 4G6

brick.books@sympatico.ca

30 Years Young
Brick Books 1975–2005

Follow the Dead Handwriting until
you come to the Hot Shoes.
Jonathan Carroll

I   The Interview   9

II   An Oak Hunch: Essay on Purdy   21

III   Mucked Rushes   49

IV   Gank Pluck   63

V   Index of First Lines   83

I
The Interview

from potscrape to yawnmouth by fridgelight

AS OF OLD

a ghost haunts a house you've lost
buy the house back—feed the ghost

a pillow & a snore outbid the going rates
a living ear is what a ghost eats

asleep & listening—weave a nursery
to a child tucked in tell a ghost story

"the blood on the stairs would not fade
'til the bones in the cellar were reburied

& the story told . . ."

WE WERE ALL STANDING AROUND THE CAR
impatiently waiting for him to

return so we could set out on our
picnic—at last here he comes—back from

the hotel men's room—where another
tourist has been cursing the local

government—without much tact it seems
he was just in the midst of sharing

this—running toward us—shouting in
his gossipy way—when the shot—as

he approached the running-board of the
topless touring car we had rented

had just stepped up—clutching his bundle
of belongings & a flagon of

red wine—yes shot—mistakenly—it
was later reported—through the back

—we took that wine along with us in
the roadster—miraculously it

had fallen on its weighted bottom
into the thick gravel—unbroken

PERHAPS THOSE CARS—ALL WIND & HORSE-HAIR
weren't called roadsters—also from the grass

of the boulevard (the long delay)
I rescued into my shawl—*this*—which

had been thrown clear—scattered—his bundle
of war-time photographs—he appears

to have had a singular talent
—or—at least others who have perused

these photographs have ventured as much

WHERE WE WERE ALL INTENDING TO GO

that day—before the shooting I mean
I am unsure—even as to whom

the dead fellow was—I called him Old
Terry-Berry—but I'm not clear how

that came about—where we did drive to
that day was a change of plans—lovely

ALONG THE WAY TO CHEER OURSELVES WE
sang the old *Owl & Pussycat* song

sang the close of each refrain with two
distinct *t-t*s at the end—oh yes

bit of a silly trademark with us
like this—*the owl & the pussy ca*

t-t—you see—*t-t*—and we drank
our dead friend's wine—tart—thick—it made one

feel as if one's teeth were coated—then
our driver made a show of flinging

the empty flagon at a road sign
near where we pulled over to picnic

beside a little waterfall—green
wet jug-glass glared shattering—*hey*—&

the wood sign quaked as we all cheered past
it was a magical—if ruined

day that epitomizes those years

NO—I LIKE TO TELL PEOPLE THAT I'M
holding out for when they invent an

elder computer—one that tells more
than I ask—ruminates—digresses

in stories—ever the same few—wise
or absurd—each telling slightly skewed

like the stories my grandmother told
—dreadful palindromic ramshackle

come-uppance aging is—from where I
have been—to this—you see—once I was

halflit by the blackouts of war—our
wide moiling storm-breaker-fronts under-

folding ranges of green into grey
columns on grand scales—spectacular

today—a stale glass of tap water
on a window ledge in drizzle-light

—spectacular

—TIPSY & IN WHAT
I now know to have been shock—or do

I flatter myself with a modern
term—I hiked my long serge skirt in the

cutgrass and brambles beside that falls
—this will sound so strange in today's terms

(the subsequent unifications)
but honestly I couldn't recall

which country we were in—we had sung
through at least two others since morning

& why would they be shooting at an
artistic type who …

                        squatting—I thought
back to the earlier incident

& rubbed my teeth on my bunched skirt hem
—I'm still able to taste that heavy

lucky wine—I was a virgin—my
friends were beginning to call for me

back at the blanket—our lunch tottered
on ground beaten deaf & idyllic

THE WATERFALL HAD LAIN DOWN—RAPIDS
really—*un bouquet des rivulets*

an artist like Old Terry-Berry
might have proclaimed as he photographed

the shimmering ripples—or—goodness
might have said of *me* at that moment

had he been still alive—& spying
—God—one image you won't find in

his collected works that you now hold
in your hand—the water's long song fell

upon me like—blood pressure—I have
lived that roar—you might say—perhaps—I

felt *vibrantly betrayed*—or if that's
too much in the grand manner—*stunned ripe*

I'm afraid my romantic reading
habits are showing now—could we stop

TO ONE OF THOSE SHOPPING CARTS
that fold away flat—Pain—the sharpener
has attached a grindstone—a bicycle wheel
& a sewing machine treadle

a mechanism never before seen
quite—has opened its shop along my veins
to the clanging of an old school bell
in familiar threes

I must take out to it the rage
I have been hiding since I was a child
I must go salveless—a snotgoblet
without one snowfall in my whole story

such improvisation will be unholy
pull the curtain around the bed please

.

Nodes

Symons, R.D. *Where Wagons Led*. (Toronto: Doubleday, 1973).
Hagell, E.F. *When Grass Was Free*. (Toronto: Ryerson, 1964).

Levine, Philip. *Not This Pig*. (Middletown: Wesleyan University Press, 1968).

Segal, Edith. *I Call To You Across The Continent: Poems and Songs for Morton Sobell in Alcatraz, and in memory of Ethel and Julius Rosenberg, executed June 19, 1953*. (New York: A People's Artists Publication, 1953).

Weiss, Allen S. "Nostalgia for the Absolute: Obsessions and Art Brut". *Parallel Visions—Modern Artists and Outsider Art*. (Los Angeles: Princeton University Press, 1993).

II
An Oak Hunch: Essay On Purdy

where wagons led when grass was free

SAYING A LOST PATH BACK

each evacuated tread cancelling a labelled dig
each bounding hoof-track deep as a nostril

a path contorting like a storm rudder
or a knob on a dash—ingrown by scrub-hawthorn

deak—waree-ree-ree—tchee—tchee

bobolinks fluffing in quillwork shadow
haw-hips detonating clay red in cold bills

guernicas of scythed footage boiling
in the soup of the day—jacklit by vagrant strobes

deflective-ornery path back
still—I'm going

IN THESE PROVINCIAL JERKWATERS
turnpiked by eagles

his carbon & foolscap
local Legion
                o wouldst thee lyrics

(stumbling in dark plowed-under cornfields

widening & falling—in arrogance with flaws
 dismissively monumentous)

glance against the sublime!

he discovers sublime limestone
where all of the old surveys wallow white

BETWEEN THE BODY & LANGUAGE
a ravine of call & response

if you look down the well for the moon
your head eclipses the shine

hurting myself is a still they'll never find

HIS COCKY DEFIANCE DROPS AWAY
increasingly awe is its own music

a surety of doubt-tone visits
after years of homemade laments & elegies

his Opeongo eyes take in & translate
a petrified flaming tongue's filibuster

when are you coming down again

how are you getting on with the two new ones

WIND IS RIPPING THE SKY'S ELUSIVE KEELS INTO BANDAGES
(armadas of realty kiting glimpses of shore)

once when these woods were new fields grunted bare
& fenced with their own charred stumps

this brambled foundation held a small barn whose roof
was the sky's only up-ended keel for leagues

THE TRAILS HE CHOPPED NORTH FOR OUR COLONIES
of inattention (Romanticism as History's axe)

stop behind us now—hacked markers—a pile of stanchions & cables

staggered images—almost *mayday*—perhaps caught

NOW EVERY JACK LIAR & THIEF
reflected in the black granite

gravestone of *the voice of the land*
reads "book" as "voice's tomb"

& carries home some keepsake
(a stone or cement chicken)

the giant & I went way back
he gave me this before he died

but thrown stones are talking
stolen cement chickens are talking

the land's voice sacred noise
thunder & lightning unlike us

DO NOT TELL ME WHAT IS GREAT
or how great gets made

tell me reknown has no split hoof
madness is privacy past its expiry date

tell me how the world can cripple
what should have been great-in-its-way

how form is the coward's defense against colour
beauty a roost

tell me how to bend lack
into a merit of language

a church-&-beans lingo
woven on surrural looms

don't show me how to growl & eat
coached eggs

THE HARDWOOD BUSH IS FALLING DOWN INSIDE ITSELF
to get a message out to the road—as if decay were cursive

a cuneiform going faster seems to help us read
thank you for being so prompt & faithful

Bill & Robin have each caught a fish

SHOCKED AWAKE
by a speck of red on a white A

woodpecker
on the slushy tin roof of this unfinished A-frame

wrong with gusto
now both of us hammering away   *damn radio plays*

blood untribalized—territories amplified
art a quirk-of-patience lingo
                              that lifts the tongue of the sky

there is always a better thunder
pending than gatling   *but gatling pays*

& THIS CLANKING KNOT OF CAST IRON
we have tugged from under edgings & brush

is a linked ladder—each rung
(once red—bent white on an anvil)

hooks into the rung above—choiring
(in Presbyterian steam & Orange Lodge water)

a finished form stood on as "good works"

A COVETED PATCH OF BATTLE TARTAN
all-seeing through its one mothball

(wave-crests were the shoulders of porters)
sang *Kiss the Barrister's Wig For Me, Pegeen*

later—scraped of hedge-row memory
silent we ate a maple darning egg fried in soot

HERE IS A CORNCOB PIPE FOR LIGHT
& two green dice for prayer

now get in this Tin-Lizzy-wingèd chariot
coursing ever south in a wide defrosting arc

its team mismatched—a killdeer
& an owl—pulling at odds

into the ghosty uncircuited realms

THIS DILAPIDATED CUTTER COULD BE
a final servant in battered skates—begging

its horsehair brow to the barn floor—grovelling
its spindle-stumps outstretched before it—*harness!*—*mercy!*

only hobbies teaming between

this is the story of how we bought the farm

FROM THE FORLORN BOWS OF THE NORFOLK PINE
from spent wet dishrags cauling spouts

each line with one end solidly pinned
penned to *in* the past

above a chasm we have crossed

FROM POTSCRAPE TO YAWNMOUTH BY FRIDGELIGHT
where wagons led when grass was free

they came like swallows to the private sea
behind each wounded migrating line

an angry mob of basted journals

ABOUT UNTO WITH FOR BY FROM
the sinews of the untoward glories

a half-ton stalled on the service road
plastic careening in factory mesh

a morning-long smoker's stare
that is Social Work's closed coffin

on top (instead of a photo) is propped
the 3-subject lined notebook of Kells

full of not once a recognizable letter
just wave on wave of careful scribbling

KNOWN SLUICES—*YOU HE SHE I IT*
promenading in a grand chain

sandbagging the allemande
what won't flush—heal—forget

anti-gung ho—gestetner purple
"dip for the oyster, dive for the clam"

TO WHERE LITTLE BAGPIPE LUNGS OF SEAWEED
pump up in the sun to hang from cords

whose switches click but bring no light
to exile from panic offshore pounding

through calm into sediment—sentiment
what I said I meant

THEY CLIMBED THESE RUNGS TO SHOVEL CROW TRACKS AWAY
or hammer themselves into early graves

adrift under second growth timber now—this copse
& us in it unmangling their ladder

A CHASM WE IN THE TALKING CLASSES
like to *think* we have crossed

(a causm
we have crassed)

TO AN OAK HUNCH
add cream of dandelion

then Chaucer Shakespeare & Clare

(barefoot light down the fresh-cut furrows
& the smudged folios)

THIS WOUNDED ROUTE—THIS DISCONTINUED LOCAL TRAIN

all the lost folk arts in the burnt bones on the wind
 cannon fodder & our own bones interlocking

a field memory whose roots are nests
 a barn memory whose thrown stooks loft

SHORTCOMINGS'LL POLISH A VOICE
(before wearing it thin)   *lineseed oil*

flaws'll buff up like treasure-knots in wood

where were groping arms
behold shining eyes   *soundpaper*

WE ARE CALLED OUT FROM SAFETY

to assist at the birth of a roaring hindsight
  that will warm us years from now

when antique tools poke
  birch kindling from the ice storms

we've licked

(OR YOU HUNTING TANGO SHOES IN GOODWILL

& waiting between your breasts
                                        a tiny black box

  migrations of granite
  had bothered grooming all my thumbs

  to unsnap like a seat-belt)

WE HAD TO LOVE TO MEMORIZE
                                        a crisp *should*

  but who tasted first to prove to any of us
    wayfarers-in-chamber—that wild is nourishment

  not the compulsory wall of books
  but one book *might*

  Wild Plums In Brandy
  (Toronto: McGraw-Hill, 1962)

  as rifled into ingredient-blossom
    as a kitchen cupboard

  one woman—Sylvia Boorman *might*
  seem to
                gathering & boiling local flora

  straining camouflage through cheesecloth
    for its jelly

OUR CHARRED TIN SONGS ALL MAP

one flagrant mucking in a noisy river
of journalism & spelling bees

                              Shakespeare
an ambulance dispatcher's one pretense

Clare a hole in the fence of a game preserve
Chaucer a midwife's balm

mix chokecherries & milkweed pods
emu oil & elderberries

A GRANDFATHER DAGUERREOTYPED—UNHANDLED—WHO
whose—his pike-pole & hobnails on the current but no one log

now stuck flow—so log jam blasts
to aim flaws we can't hook or get on without

emulate his mute dash millward
over the falls collaged photo-fries leaning

EACH TIME THE TRAIN SQUEALS TO A STANDSTILL

the conductor stops playing his autoharp
to announce how long we have (or thereabouts)

when are you coming down again

I get off & walk through each village
until I come to a bypass—a crossroad

a population sign donated by a funeral home

how are you getting on with the two new ones

WE ARE LOST AT SEA IN A WAR OF AIR
as our ancestors on that barn roof were

but now this old ladder that got them up there
anchors between us as solid as the day it was forged

OLD DUMBWATER STILL RUNS THROUGH MEMORY'S WHISTLE-STOPS

to wedding day kitchens in the basements of the eye
where *yes* has always been salt

WHEN I TURN TO HURRY BACK
it is always raining dry ink threads

curtains of penmanship—attic-holiday sighs

scrawled cursive grabs at my suit
how do you like "My Delight"

inside every map-point—a fairgrounds

stockyards have waylaid the time of day
the month & year stuffed bleatless

THE AUTOHARP CLAWS THROUGH IMPATIENT STEAM

Bill & Robin have each caught a fish

thank you for being so prompt & faithful

BUT ONE LITTLE DISTORTED GREY OFFICE EEL OF DIALOGUE
harnessed ocarina thin
                         druiding among partitions

THE FIRE TOOLS LIVE ON AS COLD GAMES IN OUR MOUTHS
soon ash

 a Milky Way of die-dots
(Mallarmé's *Un coup de dés*)

WE *ARE* WOUND *IN* BY *FROM* HOW *THE* OUT*SKIRTS* SUR*VIVE*
(it took proving the world was round to flatten it)

PITY WHAT IS LEFT OF US & OUR COUNTRY
as we dismantle & burn for cheap warmth

the guy-tropes he brought forward on his back
to get us here & past here

STOP—IN A DARK FIELD

his white shirt—jacklit—glows
 tails out among stones

a white shirt & a hockey stick
 whacking rocks into the trees

then stopping to listen

FROM HIS NAME
that made no bones

come a little fried mustardy smell
of put-out candle

FROM HIS SIGNATURE
that would have rather drunk muddy water

come a white shirt wind-loosed from a line
some dusk

its moment
of glider-starched thespian creams

caught straining ordinary days
for curds

FROM THE LONG FEUD HE MEDIATED
between *am* & *I*

 (*am*'s lemon–light
I's gull-beseech)

 come anonymity's rusty old blunderbuss
this ornate *we*

ARE BEING CALLED IN
from the dark & the damp of the night

 but to where
                        the voice is coming from
stones & cement chickens are flying

 like pucks past bedtime
through leaves & landing to not move

 for another 2000 years or so
if ever again

 (well—to not *be* moved—while whirring inside
& turning with the planet—& circling the sun)

THE FALL WIND RUSHING THROUGH THE DRY CORN
in all of the cornfields for miles around here

the paper applause of an ancient voice
that has just come around with some news

the roll-your-own salvos of the wind in the corn

a standing ovation surrounding each farmhouse

sh bravura sh

THE VAUDEVILLE PREEN OF ARTICULATION
then silence's rotten potato smell breathed in

IT IS THE SOUND OF LEAVES BEING TORN
from the dark by slapshot stones—calling

the cluck & thud of meteors broadside alighting
in mulch—once leaves—calling

it is the dark calling that calls & responds

deak—waree-ree-ree—tchee—tchee

COME IN RIGHT THIS INSTANT

no two ways about it now get in here
 you heard me

no

A CHAINSAW HAS GONE OVER

on this still-fragrant—stretched hide
page—this tightly rolled end of scroll

whose other end is tentacles
this stage where no one else has stood

stand—now—stumped
& looking down into the blue tick's whirlpool

(your library a ship's mast cut & stacked)
compose a prayer to carbon's clench

the lost path to the deep little well
said

Nodes

Austin, Leona M. *Wooler 100 Years: Through the Lens of a Camera.* (Belleville, Ontario: Mika Publishing, 1975).

Shaw, S. Bernard. *The Opeongo: Dreams, Despair and Deliverance.* (Burnstown, Ontario: General Store Publishing, 1994).
Finnigan, Joan. *Life Along the Opeongo Line: The Story of a Canadian Colonization Road.* (Manotick: Penumbra Press, 2004).

Nihilist Spasm Band, R. Murray Schafer.

III
Mucked Rushes

they came like swallows to the private sea

I'M ONLY HALF-HERE
& angry/quiet

all winter I've looked out at my little croissant-shaped balcony
& seen a pregnancy fenced—empty

the bare soft maple creaking over
is a sketched placenta the starlings use for a springboard

when I shoot in a dream—shuttlecocks lob & bounce off helmets

between resistance mountains & an iconed drop-off
I wake up—I can't make a fist

one starling with a white bib keeps pirating straw behind the cornice

I'm pretty sure it's a starling (maybe an old one or a new kind)

I MISS BEING TWO
hungers branching in synchronized plummet

rotting alone is not the flight our couple-rot knew

I wish to Jehoshaphat I'd turned too & nursed them all
humping their arses off in the flames

our blood & theirs one front against epidemic

but tell how Lot was homophobic
& for his blind eye got widowhood

lidless eyes on him among the ashes   *charvoyant*

& after midnight his own eager hand
lifting a scorched veil from a cow-lick

A NIGHT AGO THE HOOT OF THE OWL
so close & unreal—almost an imitation of itself

woke whom—what—this startled *I*
had shrunk to numb horn—a beak

a clasp on a mughole whistling oboe

defect-imperial—it—*I*—was feeding

what won't be—& *on*
what won't be

THE CHILDREN WERE LITTLE DETOURS
jumbo jets must now land on

night-lights guiding the gypsy
mountains by silent geometry

slowly down onto coasters
at 2 a.m. in a rulered doorway

their sighs crumbling
under your shadow's trowel

here is the archeology of *I guess so*
all that old slick tilt into company

has begat a parade loneliness
that can't sop up blunt longing

but is better than the long-stemmed
fists of varmints. . .

tuck a small leg under a quilt

eclipses drink from your hand

THE BIG JACK I CAUGHT IN THE STONEPILE
& put in the cellar to tame
 ran in blurred circles 'til the farmhouse spun

when I caught him again to let him go
 his hindlegs jumping in my fist like the tractor's gear knob
he tore a long furrow up the belly of my arm
 as if I'd been trying to kill myself

the house slowly stopped spinning
 & fell on its side—the cellar an open grave
its soft potatoes handled by cloud-shadow

 boy was my arm ever starting to sing

HE WAS THE SKINS OF A FEW PRIDES
each stuffed with shame

 or the skins of a few shames
each stuffed with pride

 if you figured out which
was the casing & which the filling

 he'd change them around
& you'd get hurt

 you'll get hurt—he'd warn
& look really hurt when he said it

TO WRITE TO YOU—LOVE—YEARS DEAD
to try to suck the schmaltz out of *once*

to phrase a cure at what forgets
but perhaps *love* is too strong a word

each letter a treasure map
hidden in plain view (a measure trap)

this wounded hand's itinerary
hospitalized & dying in print

or languishing cursive in the gutter of some archive
maybe *treasure* is too strong a word

maybe any word is too strong a word

DEAR LET'S NOT *EITHER/OR* ANY LONGER
but add an *e* (silent sprout) to *or*

& while we're at it honey-bunch
let's knock the dichotomy-wall down

two cohabiting's the trove
the light my head is digging for

that rare sweet *either ore*

WHEN THE DRAKE HAS MATED
his markings eclipse

liver freshettes—a basswood vein

the feathers of his green head
 ringed neck & wing bars—molting
grow back female brown

blinded—open—wider—alike

union a sacrifice of plumage
 intershuffled viscerascapes

lung bud—aspen alvioli

 on mucked rushes—alert in fatigue
not auditioning for prison or storming Codpiece Hill

 I sit the nest—guarding our cream hinge

startled—gawky/askew—growing colour back

KILLDEER

on my oozing stumps
  has drummed her wings long & hard

whipped the years' butcher block rings
  into crèche shavings

beaten nests of feathered chips
  by simulated soar

folded herself into my pages
  boatingly

her desperate ruse of broken wing
  has settled into gunwales

her closed cry
  a prow's nib

the stumps' roots
  I thought destined to be fences

are a mob of keels righting
  little brown-speckled eggs

safe—adrift—hoving-to
  as cloud-shadow swamps fields

the age of flight is followed
  by the age of sail

Nodes

Maxwell, William. *They Came Like Swallows*. (New York: Harper & Brothers, 1937).

Braden, William. *The Private Sea*. (Chicago: Quadrangle, 1967).

Holub, Miroslav. *Although*. (London: Jonathan Cape: 1971).

Howe, Susan. *The Birth-mark*. (Hanover: Wesleyan University Press, 1993).

IV
Gank Pluck
behind each wounded migrating line

HEALTH HAS NO POEM

I wade ashore—missing the stink
  petting the doctored skunk

under my breath an old tune
  we all had a hand in—all knew

What-the-Deep-Little-Well-Said Reel

SICKNESS HAD ITS BEAUTIFUL MOMENTS
each with a frozen brief glow I only half-regret

but wouldn't want my kids to have to go through
& certainly wouldn't want to trade for here now

(though *here now* sometimes seems too polished-quiet)

for sure I never want to be that 15-year-old runaway
again in 1968—lost—hitch-hiking—at the mercy

of Washington DC snow in February
after midnight drinking Bud & banana brandy

riding with this big silent black invisible driver

(a too-eager almost-health feeding on us all
& none of us really minding too much yet)

the war-lights rushing into me
in threes like pawnshop balls

WHAT WAS WRONG WITH ME BACK THEN
must have been obvious & boring—but I couldn't see it

any better than I can see what's wrong with me now

I remember I was going to write
a long poem called "What's Wrong With Me"

& there was one about Nazim Hikmet
looking out through prison bars
at a starving mule in the moonlight

something about how he couldn't name
either the moon or the mule

I forget that my rural anecdote poems & jokes
were printed in those little *gesundheit* magazines

while my crosswired lifechangers died on the table
were revised & died on the table again & again

I crawled forward—tinkering with my disfigured dead
& throwing the little square ones in the mail

I spent one whole Sunday smashing empties
with a length of pipe while the phone rang

at bottom I drank with a green-faced ogre
bus depot 2:00 a m Victoria early 80s

here was a tale I could yodel to a point
but no hole into the catacombs of the plosives

>>

instead I went foetal at the base of a tourist totem-pole
 praying *clay is the word & clay is the flesh*
but let clay waver & spout & grant my wishes

 pleading to have my runaway organs disinterred

the dog-eat-dog Boyne of the kidneys
 the bicycle tube repair kit of the alvioli
the garlic clove arrowhead fruits of the heart
 the Lorca prune of the prostate. . .

with these wet antique alphabet blocks
 I sank to my dreaded childhood landscape

that wants to look like this world but can't

or trudging—head down—reproved by cinders
  stooping between the rusted rails & the ghost towns

you'd have thought I'd lost something
  & been half-right—lost it while holding it

& found it as something else—many times

  I kept telling that shape-shifter It: *admit-omit me!*

the low foe & the wound in the frost were loud
  but the seeking was reverent play I couldn't help

you'd have thought I'd lost something upstairs

  then there was no roof but grass & the rain on it
distant multitudes—a roar full of shiny crumbling bits

  a train-wave I moved by the handful & became

I AM A WOUNDED CREATURE IMPOSSIBLE TO SEE—UNTIL
sleep charges & scatters mobs of wordplay—anthems of rhyme

   my innards are a butcher's nightmare—mobiles of pudding
I ride or do the deadman's float in a visceral parade & see

   my parents as kids wrapped in quilts that smell pissy—sockless
in rubbers in the red snow they watch themselves burnt out again

   pleated shadow-buttresses go open-gilled into flame
stiff studio portrait postcards lift pathetic fists of ash

   & I can only pretend to help
by catching in me the legendary fur-bearing trout

   when I nudge its baked fillets with my folding fork
I feather apart the soot-wafers of a burning photo album

   leaking & eating the lit parts of so many faces
lost in the life-of-the-party-until-crossed dark

THESE PRESBYTERIAN HIGHLANDS SNIFFED
indignant to be demonized by tiny limestone bones

 the pouting shadow of a fresh hole might blaspheme
twist a perfectly graceful egg-gathering hand

 to a gnarled gizzard only good for hanging a toy purse on
each Sunday—a tissue back of a clasp

 I saw Byron Lambert in the school furnace room
take off his overalls & put on a beard over his beard

 I grant each year its glowing paunch & shank
not mummery—each stark as the first years I knew here

 the Salvation Army's bushel of puzzles & molded hair
its turkey pond-hard (the blind horse's eye)—some doing

 to tenderize it all now as game—gobble—gravy—wish
get away from me with that CBC pander-mulch frippery

 the fossils in the stone piles are talking to me their chalk

I CAN HEAR MY HEART—THE CLOCK—MY BREATH
imagine pronouns metamorphosing to sea beasts

saidiment running & flapping & lifting silt—my heart's
becoming Shelley's horse—the clock's becoming Byron's

my breath almost the tide's askew crochet
little words & big Romantics gallop through me together

as in *Julian and Maddalo*—the heart or the clock is throwing a shoe
the vellum-bloused gods love to bugger up the rhythm & the key

one *here*'s stuck in a glint-pull of backwash ago

THAT'S INTERESTING—BUT RILKE
in a wool suit with a buttoned vest

is on his back in a bright garden
his trousers are down & Dolly Parton

is sitting on him—bouncing & singing
that coat of many colours my momma made for me

her mandolin-delicate fingers pinching
the points of his mustache—toy reins

without her wig or backup
she is even more homegrown-radiant

without his bookkeeper's hauteur
he is just another Bible lesson in Dogpatch

THE DAY CELAN SAW ANTSCHEL IN THE SEINE
& slipped into the ripples of the bookstalls

he rowed into the troughs of our shadows
into shadowed river bottom—into shadirt

he entered *the round Zion of the water bead*
and the synagogue of the ear of corn

(as Dylan Thomas showed us we could)
into his mother's wide eye he returned—parsed

(struck-shine fading incredulous against mire)
he sank through the curdled sheen of *Der Spiegel*   *April 1970*

to smuggle labyrinthine green
back inside grey *Kampf*ortable tongues

his cemetery-lifeguard psalms sinking in us
yellowed scrap iron pleatings of despair

the same bookstalls today along the Seine
temple gardens shattered by his repair

grubbing (suckling) into these furrows
exhume die blessing fossil

THERE IS A LIBRARY OF STRANGERS IN DUBLIN
Kraków Iqaluit Constantinople Petticoat Junction
I have borrowed two silences from—the best sleep of my life
& light moving in a Stan Brakhage film

far away at home at last
I could not be reached breached or dissuaded
I slept forever & took forever to wake up & when I did
there goes your mime teacher all in white

light was archeologizing a patchwork quilt on a bed
dusting each snag as if there were no budget constraints
the approach of the children & the long-eared goat
was a Latin declension enacted

there is a library of strangers in Dublin
the Troy-warrens of its archives boustrophedonic
silence stoops to eyeball each shard & tag it
light tests its white hands against walls in the air

(distracted indifference from the old goat & the children)

IN 1933—NIEDECKER—DRAWN DRIPPING FROM THE BACKWATERS
of Wisconsin to New York to meet—Objectivists—Zukofsky

fucked her—made her abort twins—gave her to his friend J
meanwhile lecturing how to "resolve ideation into structure"

back on Blackhawk Island she never stopped worshipping Z
in letters full of shirts & bird books doting on his son Paul

she cleaned kitchens at Fort Atkinson Memorial Hospital
for her book of poems to Paul—Z refused to write an introduction

in 1970—"I don't know what's the matter"—she said to Albert Millen
her one-armed second husband—& died loving black muck

local words—any flood—little surrealities "right down among 'em"
it makes me so goddamned angry & ashamed of what I do

& proud too . . .

OUR LITTLE CIVIC IS TOTALLED LOVE
& coming toward us out of the fog
 is the uncoupled next train of everyone
southbound to the U.S. tonight

 we can run into the cornfield
the so many stones of us lunging
 the so many hands of us clear
popping the sockets of the dry stalks

 until it seems the fog has bones
that are pioneer documents
 being shredded & then absorbed
into the fog we are gulping

 as we turn to listen to the lengthened roar
think of all the times over the years
 we have noticed our own reflections in windows
& looked away or through ourselves

 at *what is really there*
a stack of transparencies
 the stills of an animated short
two cadavers named Adam & Eve

 our first & last selves—frozen
we dyed their insides orange & blue
 thinly sliced them crown to heel
& photographed each slice

 sped up in sequence
the body comes at us like art
 as we hurtle through
listen to them all back there

>>

crying to be prized free
from the blown rust dahlias
 of the tail lights in the fog & the high beams
screening wide against cotton-batting

 soon we will hear the local sirens
& scream to be casualties among them

THE MARBLE BARGE ONE EMPRESS BUILT—WELL
had built for Her Unearthliness—surprise—sank

Mao dredged its imperial decadence up—well
his officials had it dredged up—deslimed by regiments

& set on pylons in the Summer Palace lagoon
where Yankee Dog tourists & lowly Bethune-kin

walk on it—& it seems to float . . .

I will always—well—awhile—be grateful
to the goddess of inequality—*Seems-To*

that geranium-rose resorting to rouge & gin
mother gone bad—uneaten—powdery with mould

her gank pluck keeps killing itself
in a rented room not found till the smell

the concierge & the constable pounding . . .

hewn—rock-hedged—crofts stacked
cog-dumb up Irish sea crags know her—as do

hutongs (the narrow alleys of China)—bicycle
tube roofs & broken-brick soup steaming—she is

the grin of the stuffed fox in the glass box
& the grimace of goat carcass roped in seaweed . . .

the ark of necessity's pelted hard yet
which is why we still need to be twos

keep dry & fed a dog a cat a budgie
in open doorway ramparts lean—gawk

patchwork-eyed over & out at the deluge
name it *Seems-To*—claim it *treasure*

PAINTING THE SAW—I TRY TO PUT IT TO EARNED REST
it smears—guffaws—moans eerie—snags lace

 all I've seen deserves a handle & teeth
slowly the hollow becomes the *holler* & files become *flies*

 each fresh dab is a landing light for prodigal errors
the red mailbox flag is up & the stiff chimney smoke twines

 Thomas Hart Benton—El Greco—& I
barking at a knot in barbershop harmony

 while Frankie & Johnny—St. Augustine—& Dad
lean in under a hood—conferring

 each body drawn a long wrong way that hurts loud
our lanky muscles destined for the luthier / mill

Nodes

Nicholls, Peter. "Lorine Niedecker: Rural Surreal".
　　　Lorine Niedecker, Woman and Poet. Ed. Jenny Penberthy.
　　　(Orono: University of Maine, 1996).

Stefansson, Vilhjalmur. *Great Adventures and*
　　　Explorations From the Earliest Times to the Present as Told
　　　by the Explorers Themselves. (New York: Dial Press,
　　　1947).

V
Index of First Lines
an angry mob of basted journals

AT DUSK I WOULD STOP WRITING a prayer to things
handled badly, and lifting the usual cup, snorkel
into St. James Necropolis.

FROM PLOSIVE TO DIGRAPH, from willseed to
peregrination, over the peaks of the resolute hills,
through the windows of the tall buildings, I was
alphabetizing the obvious (a chickadee—a minted
toothpick—a crying-at-bingo smell).

Saying the old, chipped words, I liked to think
I was helping *them* pray too—*words don't know
how to read, books don't know how to read—they need
my weak eyes*—I thought, like some missionary to
island lepers—but I was the one banished to an
island—and the words were the missionaries—
I am the one with these stinking wounds in the
palms of my hands—these gifts?—my articulate
hands that can not make straight arrows.

*Pity Philoctetes, ye summer boaters, who roar past his
island in your floppy hats, flinging empty beer cans at
his pines—the epauletteless shadow of the blackbird
flies out of your marshes too—its flight a red and
yellow wound, its cry a coffin hinge.*

BECAUSE OF WHAT HAD HAPPENED to me at five, a
chainsaw was talking for the trees, a witness nerve in
the brain had crimped, my bed had lost its motor and
anchor, paragraphs blurred—beneath this weak chin,
all night surf barter, bawl.

Then a white shirt would open a stone foundation, a
man would walk through half of the sun, a preacher's
motorless car would be attacked by a "rainsaw".

Don't spare me the details—I blustered—*blood fills the
peninsulas—bottom is ribbed.*

LONG BEFORE MY OWN HUNGER (for what I used not
to know), The Great Hunger had destroyed crop after
crop of my ancestors—their thin muscles looking up
through my skin like eels through ice, their dead skin
running out onto the docks of my hair, desperate for
passage—I had to eat their stories to know them, had
to plant and plow under their little songs in mine.

*While I tore eczema scabs raw in sleep, or coughed up
chunks of brown phlegm, Meatboy, whom no one saw, saw
me, his mask—intrinsic as marrow to gesture, the dry bone
fit over the eye, cousin, abuser.*

Confusing brightness with health, adventure with
trauma, torn between the self-sufficiency of epigram
and tragedy's cast of millions, I held my title pages
up to the light—saw ricocheting hairy words of hoof-
white feather flame—saw *The Great Escape* eighteen
times, *The Field* almost as often.

I'D LOST MY LAP, WAS ROAMING THE STREETS, a mess and a failure, too old, no longer believing—but I had been taught mockingbirds well, kept waking up dreaming of gods and Wagner.

Asleep in a rented tuxedo, I'd be standing in the dark doorway of a barn, listening to little outboard waves crawl up a shore—*the lake's transparent toenails* I'd mumble, pleased with myself.

"Each one of us is two stupid birds," said Killdeer (who is also Owl) when he heard that howler about the lake's toenails.

AT 14, ALL I WANTED WAS TO SEE a girl naked—then my mother died, hers an open coffin, too naked for me—now I walk on the thread of my daughter's safety, my mother's features buried and strewn—one of the names I come to: "Populi".

Originally, the 22 shell I dropped into my father's coffin was a patricide-sinker to keep him below—but it has hollowed and lightened with time, become a tiny thermos of tears, the little I can give to quench his routes.

Open my face like a tackle box on a floor beside a crib again—can't we forget this alone business—can we still recite from memory Oppen's complete *Of Being Numerous*—"the shipwreck / of the singular"—though our shared dreams have turned to faded orange?

READING MYSELF (PLANKTON) reading other men
(schools)—Neruda's hunger a kindling, Mandelstam's
candle impatiently idling (*come on, get in*), Rupert Brooke's
nude statue on Skyros a site from which to hurl my ashes
at the same Elytis blue I always wanted to paint my rented
walls.

To explain what we have done with our bodies, Serenity
comes a day late with an entourage of boistrosities, like
always—silica, the current, the stone vote translated, the
two most important words in meat, *"The Charge of the
Greys"* and greens.

Trees creaking in the wind (like doors—and me leaking
prayer), patio chairs stacked in water, our cages waiting on
rubber wheels—this has nothing to do with you, the
Absolutely Sure—nothing to do with your old purple
vinegar myth.

WHEN WE ARE SCREAMING AT EACH OTHER AGAIN,
remember the time we tried to kill hate and eat it, or the
time we tried to live above beauty on the shores of the
burrow's vision—like flies—*Y Yo Y Yo Y Yo Y Yo Y Yo* . . .

Cemetery swimmer at dawn, wrung out and shaken,
wallow-fecund—I wash our bowls and set them out
(butternut and blackthorn)—try to wave to selfyeast—hear
myself being called by a candle being blown out—*ph*.

Though we all sink back together into the masks in the
words, the anguish of balance has cost us each something
we swore we wouldn't give up for anything.

OR SOMETHING WE KNEW WE HAD TO GIVE UP if
we wanted to live—my back townships
acquiescing in the rain . . .

I hold the blunt end of the pen in my mouth,
and put my palms together so the stinking holes
in my hands make one hole I can see through.

Bowing my head, I shove the pen through the
hole in my hands—*planchette!*

SAYING A LOST PATH BACK, as of old . . .

Nodes

Johnson, Ronald. *Ark: The Foundations 1—33*.
    (San Francisco: North Point Press,1980).
Oppen, George. *Of Being Numerous.* (New York:
    New Directions, 1968).

Acknowledgements

Thanks to the editors at *The Capilano Review*
and *Event* where sections of these poems first
appeared in earlier forms.

The author is grateful for the support of the
Canada Council during these years.

The old coot on the cover is a found photo. The
wood wall he's propped on is a photo by Simon
Dragland, used by permission.

The woodcut "Sumacs, 53" on the endpapers, is
by R. T. Lambert, used by permission.

The pen & ink drawing on the section title
pages is by Gail Geltner and is also used by
permission.

Notes

The Interview

To accommodate her hesitations and age, the woman here speaks in "enneandrines"—9-beat syllabics—between the standard Greek 10 (deca) or 12 (dodeca) syllabic lines and the standard Japanese syllabic lines of 5 (go) or 7 (shichi).

This poem is dedicated to Joan Finnigan, her devotion to voices other than her own. By such devotion, to grow multi-voiced ...

An Oak Hunch: Essay On Purdy

Al Purdy read and commented usefully on an early version of this poem. The author likes to think that its finished forms retain his blessing.

Thanks to the Silversides Pioneer Tool Collection at the Rideau Canal Museum, Smiths Falls, Ontario.

This poem is dedicated to Stan Dragland, his reverence for wood & word.

Gank Pluck

"clay is the word and clay is the flesh"—the opening of "The Great Hunger" (1942) by Patrick Kavanagh.

Julian and Maddalo, by Percy Bysshe Shelley, is a gothic narrative poem that allegorizes the poet's friendship with George Byron in Italy.

"Antschel" was Paul Celan's original last name, of which "Celan" is a partial anagram, reflection.

"the round / Zion of the water bead / And the synagogue of the ear of corn"—from Dylan Thomas's poem "A Refusal to Mourn the Death, by Fire, of a Child In London".

"there is a library of strangers in Dublin"—in memoriam Stan Brakhage (1933 - 2003).

"barking at a knot"—cowboy lingo for "trying the impossible".

Index of First Lines

This poem is a boiling-off of first lines from earlier books to try to see more clearly the sub-narratives that have keeled the life—a *Windex of First Lines,* perhaps—a compacted *Selected Poems,* perhaps.

"The Charge of the Greys," a painting by Stanley Woods, depicts the brave but disastrous onslaught of the Scots Forty-Second Highland Regiment at Waterloo.

P hil Hall was born in 1953 and raised
on farms in the Kawarthas region
of Ontario. His first book, *Eighteen
Poems,* was published in Mexico City in
1973. Since then he has published nine
other books of poems, four chapbooks,
and a cassette of labour songs. Over the
years he has collected two full decks of
playing cards from the streets, as well as
numerous albums of found photographs.
He is learning to play clawhammer banjo.